Places to Go

Dona Herweck Rice

Consultant

Timothy Rasinski, Ph.D
Kent State University

Publishing Credits

Dona Herweck Rice, *Editor-in-Chief*
Lee Aucoin, *Creative Director*
Conni Medina, M.A.Ed., *Editorial Director*
Jamey Acosta, *Editor*
Robin Erickson, *Designer*
Stephanie Reid, *Photo Editor*
Rachelle Cracchiolo, M.S.Ed., *Publisher*

Based on writing from *TIME For Kids*.

TIME For Kids and the *TIME For Kids* logo are registered trademarks of TIME Inc.
Used under license.

Teacher Created Materials

5301 Oceanus Drive
Huntington Beach, CA 92649-1030
http://www.tcmpub.com

ISBN 978-1-4333-3573-0

© 2012 by Teacher Created Materials, Inc.
Printed in Malaysia.
Thumbprints.44180

Here we go!

We can go to a farm.

We can go to a beach.

We can go to a
mountain.

We can go to a
forest.

We can go to a
zoo.

We can go to a
store.

We can go many places.

We can go!

Words to Know

a	many
beach	mountain
can	places
farm	store
forest	to
go	we
here	zoo